My Little Book of
Trains

by Rod Green

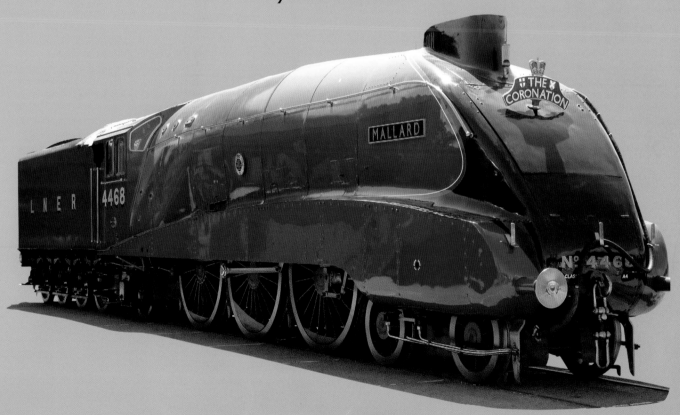

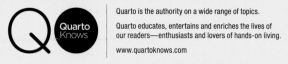

Quarto is the authority on a wide range of topics.
Quarto educates, entertains and enriches the lives of
our readers—enthusiasts and lovers of hands-on living.
www.quartoknows.com

Publisher: Maxime Boucknooghe
Editorial Director: Victoria Garrard
Art Director: Miranda Snow
Project Editor: Sophie Hallam
Design and editorial: Tall Tree Ltd

Copyright © QED Publishing, Inc. 2016

First published in the UK in 2016 by
QED Publishing
Part of the Quarto Group
The Old Brewery, 6 Blundell Street, London N7 9BH

www.quartoknows.com/brand/979/QED-Publishing/

All rights reserved. No part of this publication may be reproduced, stored in a retrieval system,
or transmitted in any form or by any means, electronic, mechanical, photocopying, recording, or
otherwise,without the prior permission of the publisher, nor be otherwise circulated in any form
of binding or cover other than that in which it is published and without a similar condition being
imposed on the subsequent purchaser.

A catalogue record for this book is available from the British Library

ISBN 978 1 78493 462 0

Printed in China

Words in **bold** are explained in the glossary on page 60.

Contents

What is a train?

A train is a big vehicle that travels along tracks. Trains carry people or **cargo** from one place to another.

⌃ **The locomotive is joined to carriages by a** coupling.

The engine that pulls a train along is called the **locomotive**. Anything pulled by a locomotive on rails is called **rolling stock**.

« **Trains that pull cargo are called** freight trains.

« A high-speed passenger train pulls out of Frankfurt Station in Germany.

Railway tracks

Trains move along railway tracks on wheels. The tracks are made from two **parallel** lines of steel rails.

⋁ **Railway tracks often cross bridges known as viaducts.**

⌄ The rails are laid down using special track-laying machines.

Each rail is about 20 metres long. They are connected to one another in parallel lines. The distance between the parallel lines is called the **gauge**.

≫ Signals tell the train driver to change tracks or change speed.

Early trains

The first trains were pulled by horses. Locomotives with engines were first used in the 1820s in the UK. The engines were powered by **steam**.

˅ This is a replica of the *Rocket*, a famous early steam train built in the UK.

⌃ **Before steam engines, horses pulled wagons along tracks called wagonways.**

The *Rocket* ran between Liverpool and Manchester in northern England from 1829. Steam trains were faster than horses and could travel further. Trains transformed the way people travelled.

Steam trains

Steam locomotives are big, heavy and noisy. They burn coal, and puff out huge amounts of dirty smoke.

« Feeding the engine with coal is hot, hard work.

Two people are needed to drive a steam locomotive. One person controls the train's speed. The other person feeds the engine with coal.

» A steam train's wheels are turned by power from the engine.

« This old steam train in South Africa is still in service.

11

Railways in Europe

By the late 1800s, railways carrying steam trains had been built to link most parts of Europe.

« Tall viaducts were built to carry trains across deep valleys and through mountains.

Big, grand stations were built for the new train services. The stations often had clock towers to tell passengers the time.

« **Bristol Station in the UK opened in 1840.**

13

US railways

In the USA, a railway linking the east coast with the west coast was completed in 1869. Called the First Transcontinental Railroad, it connected the Atlantic Ocean with the Pacific Ocean.

The line, which was more than 3,000 kilometres long, connected the older eastern US **rail network** to San Francisco in California.

« Bridges were built using wood.

« This photo shows workers laying track in Oregon, USA.

❯ **Steam trains like this Union Pacific 844 travelled on the Transcontinental Line.**

Diesel trains

Diesel locomotives are powered by a diesel engine. Diesel is a type of fuel made from oil.

During the 20th century, diesel trains replaced steam trains in most parts of the world. Diesel trains were faster and cheaper to run.

>> **This train is being pulled by two diesel locomotives, one behind the other.**

>> **This British diesel train operates at speeds of over 200 kilometres per hour.**

43058

Electric trains

Electric locomotives have engines that are powered by electricity. Most trains today are electric trains.

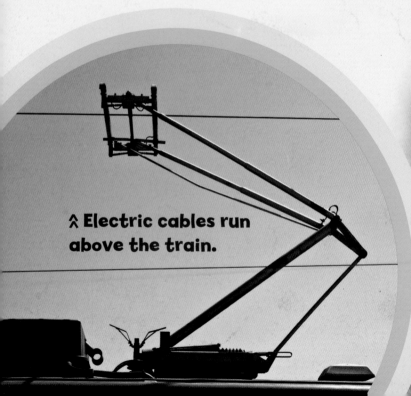

⌃ Electric cables run above the train.

>> Electric trains do not produce smelly fumes like diesel trains.

The electricity comes from a **cable**. The train needs to stay in contact with the cable to keep moving.

Bullet trains

Bullet trains are super-fast electric trains that carry people on long journeys. Japan has the longest system of bullet trains in the world.

« **The trains have long, bullet-shaped noses at the front.**

In Japan, bullet trains are called Shinkansen trains. The **top speed** of a Shinkansen train is 320 kilometres per hour.

⌃ Shinkansen trains are very safe. Accidents are avoided because no other trains travel on the same tracks.

Tilting trains

Pendolino trains are fast trains that can tilt when they travel around corners.

These high-speed trains connect big cities. They can carry large numbers of passengers in a comfortable, smooth ride.

>> Poland opened a new Pendolino service in 2014. Its trains travel at 200 kilometres per hour.

<< Passengers board a Pendolino train in Lancaster, England.

^ On tight corners the train tilts, so it does not have to slow down as much as other trains.

Trams

Trams are narrow trains that carry people around cities. They share the roads with other vehicles.

>> Passengers press a button to tell the driver to stop.

<< With 250 kilometres of track, the tram system in Melbourne, Australia, is the longest in the world.

Trams are powered by electricity from overhead cables. They travel along fixed **routes**, picking up passengers as they go.

⌵ Trams stop at regular intervals along the streets of Vienna, Austria, to let people on and off.

Rathausplatz, Burgtheater
Doppelhaltestelle 17

STRASSENBAHN
HALTESTELLE

720

D Nußdorf

720

Cable cars

San Francisco, USA, has special trams pulled by cables. They carry passengers up the steep roads.

The cars are pulled by cables that run below the street. The cars run at a constant speed of 15 kilometres per hour.

^ **The cables are pulled from a power house above ground.**

>> **Passengers can stand on a platform outside the carriage.**

The drivers are known as grip operators.

Funicular railways

>> This funicular has been carrying people up and down a hill in Budapest, Hungary, since 1870.

Funicular railways carry passengers up very steep slopes. The trains are pulled up the slope by a cable.

Funicular trains work in pairs. One train climbs the slope while the other goes down the slope. The two trains balance one another.

>> A funicular in Karlovy Vary, Czech Republic, has been in service since 1915.

28

Monorail

A monorail is a train that moves along one track. The track carries electricity, which powers the train.

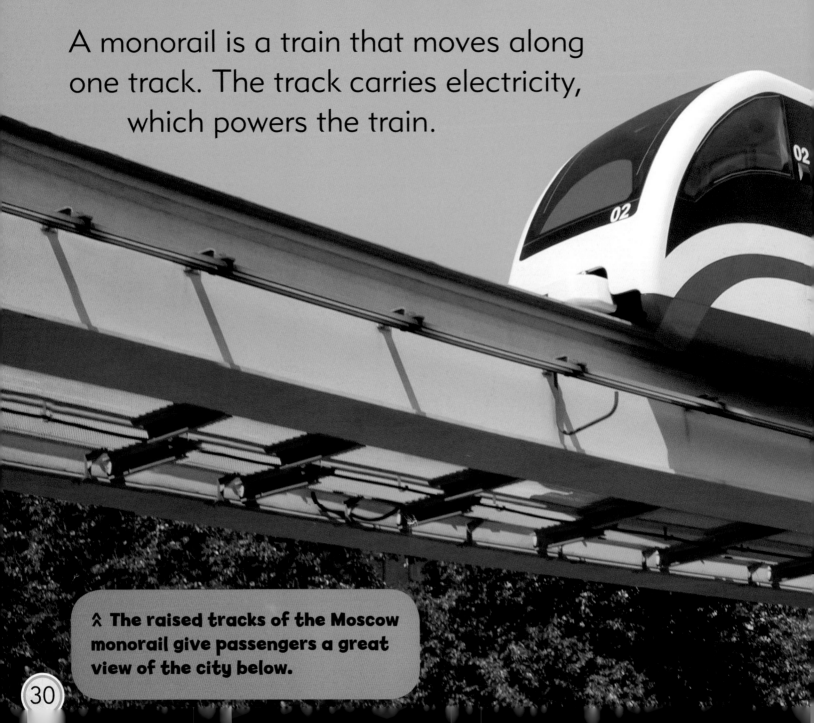

⌃ **The raised tracks of the Moscow monorail give passengers a great view of the city below.**

Monorails are found in cities. The tracks are raised up so that the trains can pass above other traffic.

>> The Okinawa monorail is one of ten monorails in Japan - more than in any other country.

Maglev trains

Maglev trains are trains that are powered by **magnetism**. They are the fastest trains in the world, travelling at more than 400 kilometres per hour.

« The first maglev service opened in Shanghai, China, in 2004.

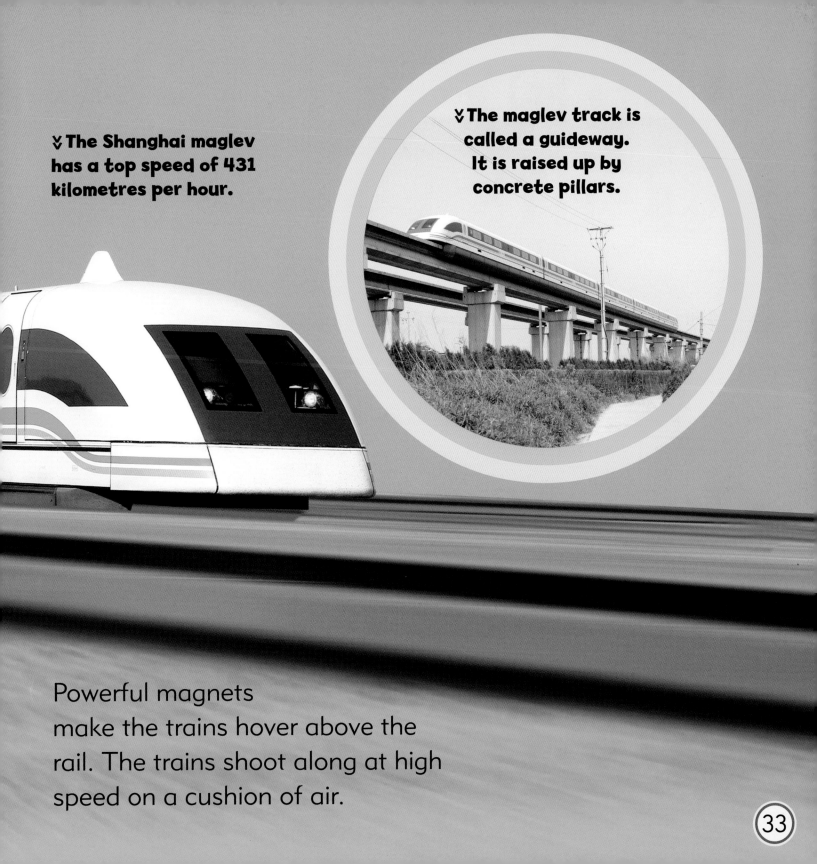

❯ The Shanghai maglev
has a top speed of 431
kilometres per hour.

❯ The maglev track is
called a guideway.
It is raised up by
concrete pillars.

Powerful magnets
make the trains hover above the
rail. The trains shoot along at high
speed on a cushion of air.

Underground trains

Many big cities are served by underground trains. The trains move through a network of deep tunnels.

The trains get busy in the mornings and evenings when people are travelling to and from work. These busy periods are called 'rush hours'.

>> **The** metro **in Tokyo, Japan, is one of the busiest in the world. Every day it carries nearly 7 million passengers!**

» During the rush hour on the Toronto underground, many passengers have to stand.

^ The London Underground is the oldest underground rail network. It opened in 1863.

Commuter trains

Commuter trains carry people to work. They link the **suburbs** with city centres.

❖ **Many commuters work while they're travelling on the train.**

« In Indonesia, people sit on the roofs of really busy trains.

Commuters are people who live in one place and work in another. They need reliable trains to get them to work in the morning, and home in the evening.

⌃ This commuter train in Slovakia is a double-decker.

Freight trains

Freight trains carry cargo rather than people. They carry heavy goods over long distances.

⌃ **Coal is often transported on long freight trains.**

⌃ **Five diesel locomotives combine to pull a long line of containers full of cargo across the USA.**

Powerful locomotives are needed to pull the heavy loads. Freight trains usually travel slowly as they are so heavy.

« Large freight trains often use a wide-gauge track to spread the heavy load.

Shunters

A shunter is a small locomotive that moves carriages over short distances.

˅ Most shunters have diesel engines.

Shunters are used to bring carriages together, ready for a larger locomotive to take over. They can also push large trains to help them to start.

˄ Shunters are powerful but have a low top speed.

Engineering trains

Engineering trains (work trains) are used to build or repair tracks. They can also clear tracks of obstacles such as fallen trees.

>> **This train in California, USA, is building a wide-gauge freight track.**

REG006 KBR 875

« This train in Romania is clearing snow from the station.

Railway tracks need to be in top condition for trains to run safely. Engineering trains can check the track for signs of damage.

» This car and the carriage it pulls use electronic equipment to examine the rails for cracks that are too tiny to see.

Tourist trains

Trains are a great way to see **scenery**. Sightseeing trains travel slowly, allowing the passengers to enjoy the view.

>> Sometimes, old steam locomotives pull carriages. This one is in Anduze, France.

>> **A narrow-gauge train carries visitors along the coast in North Wales.**

SOUTHERN 759

040 T 1751

Some old train lines are run by volunteers. Train **enthusiasts** repair old trains and run the lines for fun.

>> **Open-air carriages give a great view.**

Fastest trains

The fastest train in the world is the new Japanese maglev. In test runs, it has hit a top speed of more than 600 kilometres per hour.

When it goes into service in 2017, the train will connect the cities of Nagoya and Tokyo. It will cover a distance of 290 kilometres in just 40 minutes.

>> The train is being tested on a specially built track.

∧ The world's fastest steam train was the *Mallard*, a UK passenger train that was in service until 1963. It had a top speed of 200 kilometres per hour.

Longest trains

The longest trains of all are freight trains. Some Canadian freight trains are more than four kilometres long.

The trains travel at an average speed of 50 kilometres per hour. At this speed, it takes five minutes for the whole train to pass by.

⋁ **These huge trains carry containers stacked on top of one another.**

« This train
in Australia
is the longest
passenger train
in service. It
can have up to
99 carriages.

Miniature railways

Miniature railways are smaller versions of the real thing. They are operated in tourist areas to give a fun, open-air ride.

« Theme parks often have miniature railways.

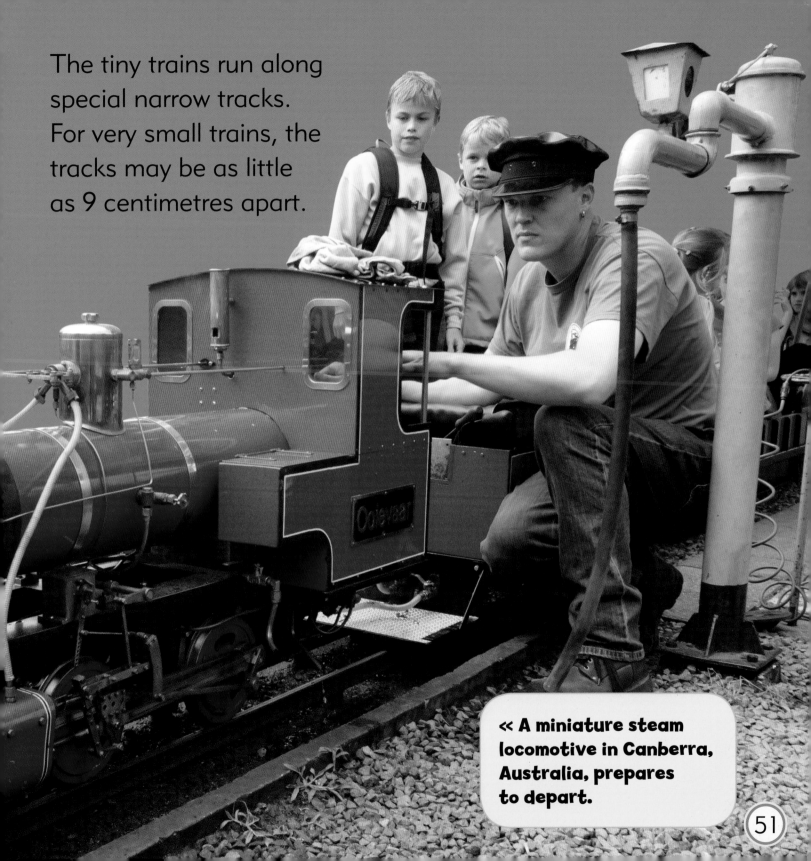

The tiny trains run along special narrow tracks. For very small trains, the tracks may be as little as 9 centimetres apart.

« A miniature steam locomotive in Canberra, Australia, prepares to depart.

Sleeper trains

Sleeper trains are passenger trains that travel long distances. The carriages are fitted with beds so that passengers can sleep during the journey.

In luxury sleeper trains, the beds are usually stored overhead. When the passengers want to go to sleep, they pull the beds down.

« Passengers can relax in the lounge car.

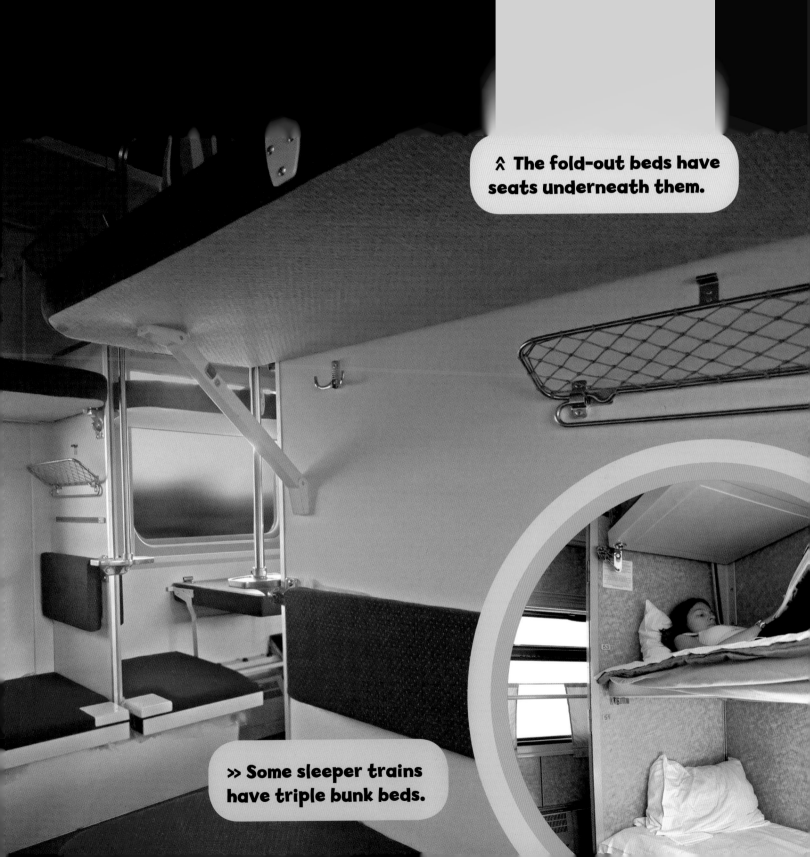

⌃ The fold-out beds have seats underneath them.

≫ Some sleeper trains have triple bunk beds.

Luxury trains

Passengers who want to sit in extra comfort travel **first class**. Passengers who want a **luxurious** journey may travel on a luxury train.

One of the most famous luxury trains is the Orient Express, which travels from London to Venice. It has carriages dating from the 1920s.

« **A conductor welcomes passengers aboard the Orient Express.**

« A waiter prepares a table in the dining car of the Orient Express.

Bridges and tunnels

The oldest train tunnels and bridges are in Europe. The biggest and newest are in China. China is home to the longest railway bridge and the longest rail tunnel in the world.

« This iron viaduct in France was built in 1885.

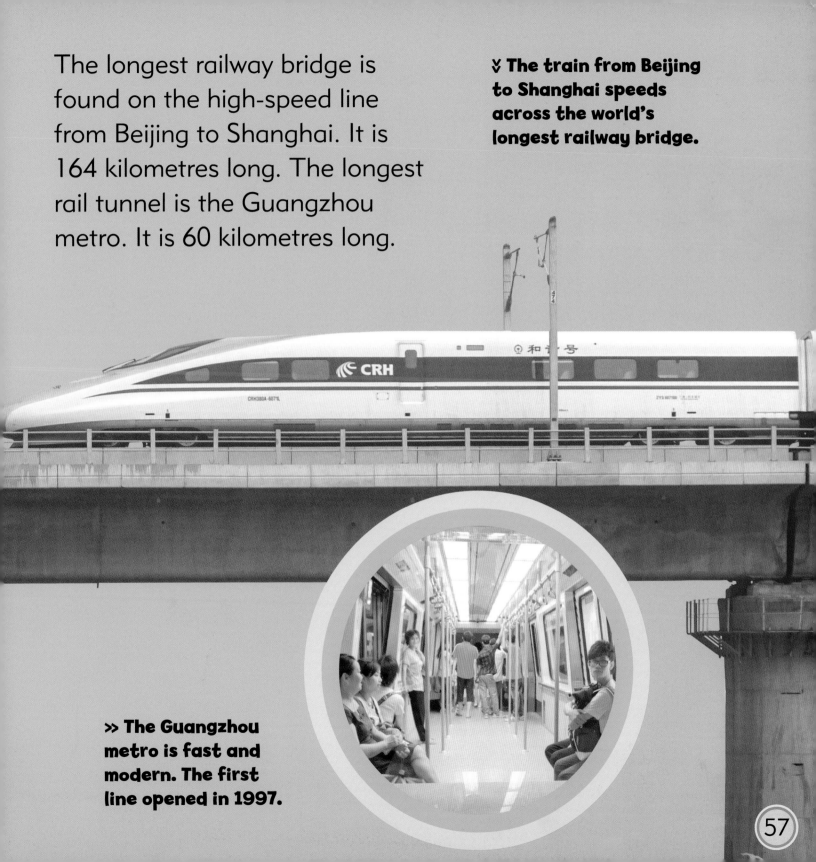

The longest railway bridge is found on the high-speed line from Beijing to Shanghai. It is 164 kilometres long. The longest rail tunnel is the Guangzhou metro. It is 60 kilometres long.

˅ **The train from Beijing to Shanghai speeds across the world's longest railway bridge.**

≫ **The Guangzhou metro is fast and modern. The first line opened in 1997.**

Future trains

In the future, trains may zoom through special tunnels at speeds of more than 1,000 kilometres per hour.

In California, USA, scientists have built a five-kilometre-long tunnel to test their new ideas for super-fast trains. The project is called Hyperloop.

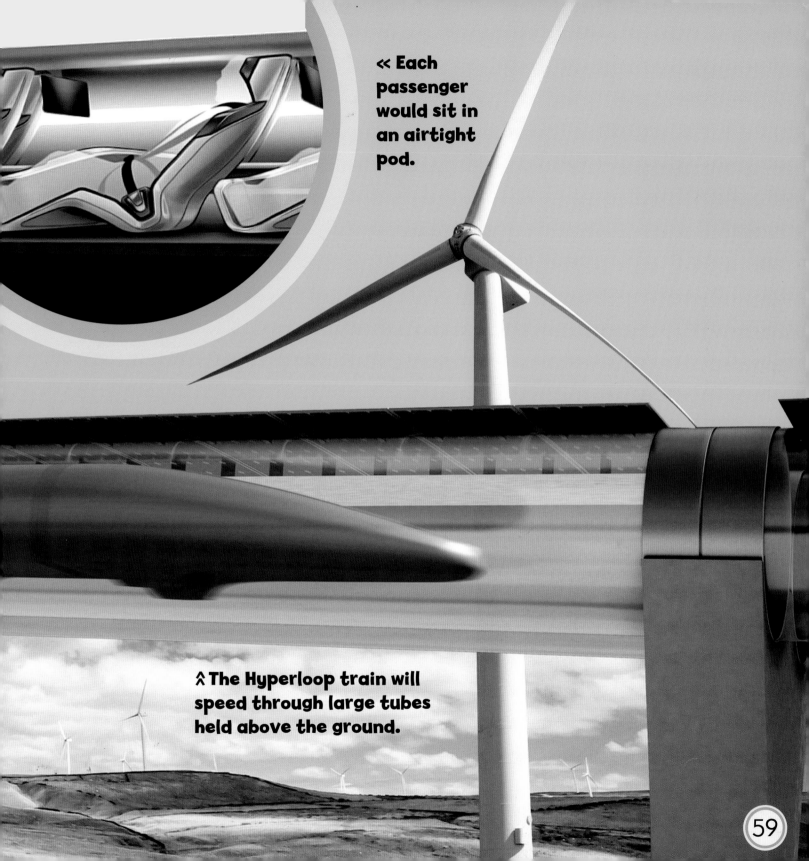

≪ Each passenger would sit in an airtight pod.

⌃ The Hyperloop train will speed through large tubes held above the ground.

Glossary

cable A type of wire. Electric trains get their power from an overhead electric cable.

cargo The load a vehicle carries, such as coal or mail.

conductor The person who inspects the passengers' tickets on a train.

coupling A device for connecting the carriages of a train.

diesel A liquid fuel, made from oil, used in diesel engine trains.

dining car A carriage in which passengers sit to eat meals.

enthusiasts People with a keen interest in something, such as old steam locomotives.

first class A section in a train with comfortable seating. To sit in first class, passengers must buy a first-class ticket.

freight trains Trains that carry cargo, not passengers.

gauge The measurement between the two rails of a track.

locomotive The vehicle that pulls the carriages of a train.

lounge car A carriage selling snacks and drinks.

luxurious Something that is very high-quality and often expensive.

magnetism A force created by magnets. Maglev trains use magnets to glide over the track at very high speeds.

metro A train network that serves a city. A metro may be part above ground and part below ground.

parallel Lines separated by a constant distance. Train tracks have parallel rails.

rail network A connecting system of railway lines

rolling stock Carriages and trucks that are pulled along railways by locomotives.

route The direction a train or tram travels. Routes are usually fixed, so passengers will know where and when to board.

scenery The natural features of a landscape, such as fields and mountains.

service The route, timetable and train facilities offered by a train company.

steam Water that has turned into gas. A steam engine uses a coal furnace to boil water and create the steam that powers the engine.

suburb An area where people live, outside of the city.

top speed The highest speed a vehicle can travel.

Index